While Looking Out at the Bay

Arthur Bull

© 2022 Arthur Bull

All rights reserved. No part of this book may be reproduced or transmitted in any form or by any means, electronic or mechanical, including photocopying, or by any information storage or retrieval system, without permission in writing from the publisher.

Cover image: Arthur Bull
Author photo: Charles Bull
Cover design: Rebekah Wetmore
Editor: Andrew Wetmore
ISBN: 978-1-990187-49-0
First edition October 2022

2475 Perotte Road, Annapolis County, NS B0S 1A0

moosehousepress.com
info@moosehousepress.com

We live and work in Mi'kma'ki, the ancestral and unceded territory of the Mi'kmaw People. This territory is covered by the "Treaties of Peace and Friendship" which Mi'kmaw and Wolastoqiyik (Maliseet) People first signed with the British Crown in 1725. The treaties did not deal with surrender of lands and resources but in fact recognized Mi'kmaq and Wolastoqiyik (Maliseet) title and established the rules for what was to be an ongoing relationship between nations. We are all Treaty people.

Also by Arthur Bull

Books
Key to the Highway Roseway Editions (2000)
The Lake Diary Emmerson Street Press (2010)
Fifty Scores teksteditions (2015)
Blue Mat–Poems After Yang Wanli Anaphora Press (2017)
Division Street Hidden Brook Press (2019)
One Hundred Sonnets (2021)

Chapbooks
Hawthorn Broken Jaw Press (1994)
25 Scores Runaway Spoon Press (1994)
Six Birds Origami Poems (2014)
Woodlot Another New Calligraphy (2015)
I Step into a World The Alfred Gustav Press (2019)

Other publications
Writing the Rules of Ecological Fisheries Management in the Bay of Fundy, with D. Coon and M. Recchia, Bay of Fundy Marine Resources Centre (1999)
Community Fisheries Management Handbook with J. Graham and A. Charles, The Gorsebrook Institute St. Mary's University (2006)

Doing Our Homework: Policy Change and Community Organizations, The Coastal Communities Network (2003)
Co-Management Handbook Masifundise/Coastal Links, Masifundise Trust-South *Africa (*2018)

Recordings
Solo Guitar (2000)
Peepers and Coyotes (2008)
Back Dooryard Songs (2019)
Guitar Improvisations (2021)
Handwoven (2022)

He also appears on 23 (so far) CD recordings with small groups.

For Sam and Alex

A number of people appear in this poem. You may not be familiar with them all. Check the **Mentors** section at the back to verify, for instance, whether the Marx in question is Karl or Groucho.

While looking out at the Bay

Prelude..9
Abstraction...11
Rocky shore...21
Far...33
Waves...43
Currents..53
Horizon...67
Seaweed..79
Clouds..87
Fog again..103
Tidepool..115
Coda..117
    Mentors...121
    Acknowledgements..127
    About the author..129

Arthur Bull

While looking out at the Bay

Prelude

To make a rag rug you bring in all
the stuff that you can find, from anywhere:
pajamas, silk ties, rags, aprons, underwear,
old wedding dresses, printed cotton, towels,

Tablecloths, curtains, shirts, bright scarves, and shawls.
Gather them in a heap, and then you tear
them into equal strips with exacting care
then sort by colours waiting to be recalled

And woven slowly into a whole combined
fabric like the moving surface on the Bay—
cross-hatch of currents, tides, whitecaps and waves.

Blended by sunlight, a single surface binds
so every difference subsumes into one, the way
my memories become the love I save.

Arthur Bull

While looking out at the Bay

Abstraction

You look, and the longer you look the more abstract it gets.
Fog lifts, unveiling three horizontal layers:
Sky-blue dotted with white cloud, slate-grey
flecked with whitecaps, basalt shore strewn with black
boulders. More abstract, each moving inside itself,
in its own time, each separate: rock time,
water time, sky time. How many hours
have I stared out into the Bay like this? Years?
Lifetimes?

Arthur Bull

I can't help but wonder about Leify.
Leify, who must have stared out there too,
the only person who ever lived along this shore,
just her and her brother Ben, isolated, no road
in, just a path through the woods to Tar Cove,
a shallow inlet filled with driftwood and seawrack,
a morning's walk to Sandy Cove, the nearest village.
They all said she was a witch, so they'd go see her
for herbal remedies and old cures. I always assumed
from this that they were Mi'kmaq, but later I learned
they were in fact English, West Country folk.
How they got here to the end of the world, tossed up
on this shore, is a tale no one will ever hear.
She seldom came to the village, they said, and when she did
the children would tease her because she would never
ever step over a line. 'Bad luck,' she always said.

While looking out at the Bay

So they would draw a line in the dirt with a stick
to make her walk around it. When Leify died
they said they only found her after five days and Ben
was just sitting there saying nothing.

Now I imagine
her spending hours looking out at the Bay staring,
reading into the patterns of whitecaps, clouds, seagulls,
tides, interlocking iron lines in the basalt, rockweed
all the long scrolling of sentences speaking in a kind
of wild code. Pointless now to speculate about that,
but hard not to wonder as I look out there
at the three ribbons undeciphered, waiting
to be spoken aloud, each flowing. Even rock loses
its solidity, having slowed from first volcanic outpouring,
squeezed out between tectonic plates of Pangaea, bubbling,

Arthur Bull

cooling, pitted with holes from escaping gasses,
slowed now to its billion year pace, but still flowing
nonetheless although flowing is only what appears
to be happening, continuous movement inside each layer.
Abstracted from breakages, interruptions, sudden unpredictable
gestures, intermittent gaps, lacunae, splinters, distractions,
fractures, plowing itself into abstraction imposed on the brokenness
of everything.

To abstract this from that is to lift ideas from events,
draw concepts from categories, from subordinate concepts.
Or the way you could paint it as three horizontal bands,
slate grey, blue grey and light blue. Three
might be the first abstraction. Leaving out religion,
you can find it anywhere. Peirce talked about threes as a wonderful
operation of hypostatic abstraction by which we seem to create

entia rationis, that are nevertheless sometimes real, and furnish
us the means of turning predicates from being signs that we think
or think through, into being subjects thought of. We thus think
of the thought-sign itself, making it the object of another
thought-sign. Thereupon, we repeat the operation of three-fold
abstraction, and from these second intentions derive third intentions.
Does this series proceed endlessly? Peirce thought not.
What then were the characters of its different members?

Then there's abstraction in painting, we say, freed from representation,
something altogether different than Peirce's. The way you
could paint this place with a roller as pure abstraction:
three bands: dark grey, jade green and light blue,
three even areas of colour Rothko-like, across
a canvas, almost the same as the one I'm looking at now.
Is this lifting ideas from events? My confusion increases

Arthur Bull

the more I think about this kind of abstraction, without
even bringing in the historical and political kinds of abstraction.
That is, an abstraction of place needed to make it a commodity,
mapping and segmentation of space into tradeable units.
Right here, for example. To take this land away
from the Mi'kmaq to make it not only a British
possession, but also a possession of any kind, into property
at all, requires a high degree of precise abstraction
starting with mapping, laying the land on a grid, now
measurable in units of equal value, and in turn laid
on another grid, money, that is, and therefore registered
in another world system. Without this, it cannot be property,
cannot be granted, cannot be bought and sold, cannot be stolen.
It must become commensurable with money, as Marx says

While looking out at the Bay

> The commodity which functions as a measure of value
> and therefore also as a medium of circulation,
> either in its own body or through a representative is money.
> Gold (or silver) is therefore money.
> It functions as money, on the one hand,
> when it has appeared in person as gold.
> It is then the money commodity, as when it is a measure
> value, nor capable of being represented, as when it is the
> medium of circulation. On the other hand,
> it also functions as money when its function,
> whether performed in person or by a representative,
> causes it to be fixed as the sole form of value,
> or, in other words, as the only adequate form of existence of
> exchange in the face of all other commodities,
> here playing the role of use-values pure and simple.

Nothing

in all of this could predict the strange story of the mink

I encountered on the shore one sunny day down on the rocks,

where I often came one summer long ago to sit and read

on a little platform of boards I'd built, with a pile of books

Arthur Bull

and a cup of tea. For some reason, I was reading Marx that day
specifically Marx on value. I remember puzzling over the bit
about things having a use-value without being a value, and how
whenever its utility is not mediated through labour,
virgin soil, natural meadows and unplanted forests
fall into this category and how a thing can be useful and a product
of human labour without being a commodity, and how finally
nothing can be of value without being an object of utility.

Just at that point where I was struggling with what Marx
was talking about, right in the middle of one of these sentences,
right in front of me, on the rocks between the wooden platform
I'd built down there for sitting and the water: A mink
appeared, sleek, moving fast, almost flowing over the rocks,
its long body almost reptilian, and its fur in the sunlight
with a sheen and depth of blackness that explained

While looking out at the Bay

exactly its value as the prime luxury commodity in markets
from Montreal to Shanghai. Without thinking I shouted at it:
"You fuckin' scared me," nonsensically expressing my shock,
addressing it as a friend who had acted inconsiderately.
The mink took no notice of me, not even turning its head,
even though it was so close, probably thinking about some
important mink business, and then disappeared along
the rocky shore, presumably taking all of its value,
use or otherwise, with it.

> Sleek and black,
> a mink flows
> over basalt
> the way lava
> must have flowed.

And what about the value
of the fact that this place here is now and will always be

Arthur Bull

Mi'kmaki, home of the L'nu, no matter what other values have been abstracted or superimposed from elsewhere. That value remains, undivided and unmeasured.

While looking out at the Bay

Rocky shore

While I wasn't looking, a fog bank filled the Bay,
and rolled slowly toward the shore, erasing everything
before it, erasing sky and water, erasing abstraction
with greater abstraction. Now there is only margin,
all clarity of close-up framing detail as foreground:
basalt surfaces, fractal-like, the smallest
broken-off piece a mirror of giant boulders.

Years ago I wrote a poem about a painting
by Paul-Émile Borduas called "Expansion Rayonante".

Arthur Bull

      House-sized boulders
            arranged along the shore,
against the fog, shaped
               black on white
                        and nothing more
No gradual declension
         here no gentle slope
                through dusk.

Only this: what absorbs
         everything's colour
against what reflects
         everything's colour
                just black on white

And in that clarity
         they feign stillness as if
they were not really still
            hurtling outward
                  from the centre's
                          radiant blast

While looking out at the Bay

    And fool us into thinking
            that we are not going
                    with them that we are not
    also at the centre
            of that explosion.

Pocked all over with these tiny bubble holes

imprinted on the red-hot flow, a ridge that rose

into the heart of Triassic, a kind of memory

held in place by place and formed by form, recording

a long forgotten story. We have some words

we like to use to try to gain a purchase on a world

that we were never part of, except in scientific legend,

with names like the Pangaea Supercontinent,

fractured 220 million years ago,

the earth's lithosphere torn apart by stress,

that broke and shaped the borders of the plates.

A rift beginning somewhere between eastern

Arthur Bull

North America and northwestern Africa fused
by convulsive energy. Along the Mid-Atlantic Ridge,
an undersea volcanic mountain range forged
in one chthonic furnace continuously spreading.
A sequence of tholeiitic basalts, containing
and joining columnar magma flow. Basalts
cut with magnesium, feldspar, pyroxene, iron,
and hints of siliceous materials like granite.
Agates appear as nodules in the volcanic rock
or ancient lavas, in former cavities produced by volatiles
in the original molten mass, which are then filled, wholly
or partially, by siliceous matter deposited in regular layers
(Agate, that rock hounds chip and gather
then polish in slow back porch rolling tumblers).
Agate, in veins or cracks, alters rock, cutting
transversely a deep succession of parallel lines,

While looking out at the Bay

creating banded agate, riband agate, striped agate.
stillbite, heulandite, jasper, chalcedony, zeolites,
veins, patches pockets scrolls reveal resemblances
to landscapes: bare trees against wide valleys
receding into mist only the faintest outlines
of chateaux and barns floating halfway up
the mountainside. Jasper veins in deep yellow
or deep red-grey, chalcedony streaked veinlets
mottled and mixed with quartz's crystals pinkish
chocolate brown veins spreading through basalt.
What is solid and certain is that once rivers of lava
flowed along this shore.

The idea of a hard immovable reality of the rock is false.
It is still changing. Nothing is not changing,
even the hardest thing is empty of any self existence. Fragile

Arthur Bull

and fine porcelain fired in the fieriest of kilns,
floods of lava pouring up through the earth's crust
spreading, then cooling into patterned hexagons.
Splinters, tufts, time's creator's hands, threads of ritual
and refusal, human inventories that are only filaments of data
inherent in things as aesthetic choices of rocks, grinding
history along the way through a series of fusions, rupturings,
forgettings, rememberings, imprint matter on matter.
Hardness disappears, dissolving in clouds of smoke shapes
of dragons, and ascends way high over the Bay.

Awkward gestures, called sometimes chances, unfold
as subtle and ambiguous signals bypassing every filter
and obstacle. The living art of nature making art
of itself, patterning in intricate logic of crystals,
shaping huge boulders, floating on the surface.

While looking out at the Bay

Each one unique, a grandfather rock,
living beings, like sculptures by Arp or Moore.
Scholars' rocks floating like small black clouds:
The Fist of Stone, Vast, Wild Dark Clouds
Rising, Watering the Ten-Thousand Things roll up.
Lean, wrinkled, porous, or unroll in sinuous clouds,
creating caverns, hollow instruments that amplify
tide's roar, scored. Penetrated, a perfect essence
remains as form: Form is emptiness. Emptiness is form.

The Mustard Seed Garden Manual of Painting, (1679,
printed in five colours) says rocks are the roots of clouds.
Where the rocks give way to shallow soil reveals
a narrow zone of low vegetation edging the forest.
At first with seeming sameness, one low bed, all of a piece,
becomes more variegated, the closer you get: a quilt

Arthur Bull

of beach grass, cordgrass, sedge, eelgrass, sweetflag,

wild iris, goosefoot, sea lavender, birdseye,

pearlwort, beach pea, wild rose, foxberry,

punctuated by scrawny spruce trees, with all their branches

facing straight toward the land, none toward the Bay,

> In the summer heat
> that scraggly spruce
> bears witness to winter:
> the branches all point
> the same direction.

Undersong of memory and strict training of winter storms.

Following the alphabet of driftwood a little further

along the shore are scattered here and there fragments

of the *SS City of Colombo*, a steamer that ran aground

in 1921. Long squared-off beams with giant bolts,

While looking out at the Bay

wedged between boulders, and scraps of half-inch iron

from the hull, crumpled like a piece of paper.

Wreck

Steel petals scattered
along the rocks,
one inch plate
peeled back and
curling around the edges.

Fireweed's unfirey pink
crowds in around
the rusty shards.

One section lies
face down in a bog:
through the porthole
eelgrass waves
gently in a spring
where someone once
saw foamy death
One section teeter-

Arthur Bull

      totters on a boulder
      a perfect gull table
      for cracking crabshells,

      Or a drum for boys
      with driftwood mallets
      unafraid yet
      of waking ghosts

      Or a deckchair for a sunbather
      thinking of the past year's
      events and losses
      of how disaster
      eventually settles
      into the landscape

      Of what kind of force
      it took to tear
      and toss a ship
      of what laughter
      accompanied it.

While looking out at the Bay

Or the *Robert Cann*, 263-ton freighter
from Saint John that, in a sudden blizzard in1946,
springs a leak and quickly begins to take water.
For hours, the crew are storm-tossed in a small lifeboat,
exposed to the freezing winds, finally reaching shore
on an uninhabited stretch of Digby Neck.
Eleven die from exposure before reaching
land at Riley's Cove and a logging road. Two are alive,
though one is too weak to struggle through the dense
woods. Only one, Captain Ellis, finds an old lumber track
and makes his way to Lake Midway and the home
of Mrs. J. T. Dimock, who calls the RCMP in Digby.
This happened near my house at Lake Midway.
The Bay holds the memory of this event in every detail.

Arthur Bull

The fog starts coming back in, and just before
it closes around everything, a seabird enters the water
reminding me of a poem I wrote years ago:

> That Northern Gannet
> pierces the Bay's skin
> just like a syringe

While looking out at the Bay

Far

Most days the sun will burn off the fog by noon,
beating away behind it all morning, felt but not seen
until, without noticing how it happened, everything clears,
the wide Bay opens out way over to Grand Manan,
or rather to the Wolves, a chain of tiny islands, barely
visible, that emerge in the distance, sky's immensity
vaporizing light swirls and sweeps, turning *in* the sky
but not *of* it, not filling it, the water's broken edges
moving and lifting a mountain range of clouds, and there,
far on the horizon a small black rectangle, what looks like

Arthur Bull

just a black box resting on its side: an oil tanker.
Almost imperceptibly slowly moving, like a detail added,
the same way Turner would add in some minuscule object,
some reminder of another world, like the snail
in the mud at the feet of Napoleon, or the hare in front
of the oncoming locomotive, or in *Sunrise with Sea Monsters,*
the tiny buoy that tells us they're not monsters,
only a dazzling daybreak on a normal fishing day.
The oil tanker, not much more than a speck, does this,
turning the whole canvas, a luminosity of sea and sky,
endless obscurity without boundaries, waving visible
streaking diagonals leading to dark scalloped arches,
the fierce violet light clashing streams, clamour
of foam, cloud overlapping clouds, curving over gnarled
waters, whirlwind swivelling vortex of currents.

While looking out at the Bay

No wonder the poets found it terrifying, pushing them
past wonder to the actual horror of craggy peaks,
the inability to take in the whole of the oceans
or mountains, mixing anxiety and pleasure,
straining the mind at the edge of conceptuality,
Mingled with horrors and sometimes with despair
of wasted mountains and noble ruins. In some ways
all this reminds so much of the early days of LSD,
the same mixture of terror and wonder as we watched
the marks of our identities dissolve before our eyes,
the sense of being no longer either 'there' or 'here',
with hallucinations as real as what we saw or heard,
so the rug is pulled out from under us. Too much
to take in. Was this our Sublime? The fear of losing
ourselves and the control we thought we had
to something we could not encompass with our minds.

Arthur Bull

And against such a background, a miniature detail

can throw the whole thing off, and wreck the project.

> A tiny black rectangle on its side
> at once appears, distant across the Bay:
> an oil tanker that slowly makes it way
> to Saint John, a detail that elides
>
> The ocean, revealing a fact that hides
> inside the scene: the energy we say
> we need to do important things that pay:
> animals, wind, coal, nuclear, rivers, tides
>
> And slaves. Never enough to meet our needs
> we must keep drawing down and using up
> to build the edifice that history will dictate.
>
> Whatever power it will take to feed
> the habit that we have and cannot stop:
> we must have more, and that's our tragic fate.

While looking out at the Bay

And so in this way a tiny oil tanker on the horizon

changes the whole Bay by bringing in the global economy,

and specifically the world energy economy, although

that would not be new to the Bay, having seen wind,

wood, coal, tidal energy, and even human

energy: slaves—Turner's slave ship picture, surely

the source of more horror than all the sublime scenes

the world has ever seen—and then steam,

the twinkling lights of the Lepreau Nuclear Station

are a reminder of the global economy and the sublime,

The oil tanker calls up the wide opening of seascapes, posing the

question: How does the Sublime relate to Empire?

The sea's infinitude gives rise to a doctrine of
free trade well before it provides a basis
for 18th century aesthetic notions of the sublime.
Panoramic maritime space in Dutch painting

Arthur Bull

implicitly "open" in this pre-Romantic sense:
open to trade, a net cast outward upon the world that
yields property but that in its idealized totality is
irreducible to property. When protoromanticism is later
confronted by the uncommodifiable
excess, it transforms it into the sublime, taking it initially
as proof of divinity. Only later is the category naturalized and
psychologized. So says Sekula, seer of oceans.

Empire, the rape of the world, requires a sense of boundlessness,

emptiness, terra nullius. A space that must be filled.

Of course global trade was nothing new at all,

For five hundred years a system of overlapping circles,

each one with a trading city at its centre:

Bruges, Genoa, Venice, Baghdad, Malabar, Ceylon,

Zanzibar, Fuzhou, Tashkent, each staying within

its own sphere, but trading with the surrounding

spheres, woollens from Flanders ended up in Hangzhou.

While looking out at the Bay

Across Mediterranean, Indian Ocean, over Silk Road
silk went from Guandong to Burgundy the same way.
This system was disrupted when Europe changed
the game by adding domination, aggression and plunder,
not just conquering the world, but laying a grid on it.
This is a new kind of empire, that must measure all before it
to integrate it into the world capital, everything must be
laid on the mesh and sectioned off, counted and priced,
and as this happens the power of the sublime becomes more
pronounced and terrifying. What were they so afraid of?

Walking through the woods over to the Bay the constant
sense of there being more all around that I can't take in,
always trying to penetrate the woods with my eyes
and ears, always aware how shallow their reach is,
the beyond always beyond in the depth of the woods,

Arthur Bull

unreachable, scattered between the patches of emerald
green moss and the last remaining not yet melted
snow—tracks of rabbits, coyotes, deer, bobcats,
partridges, but never seeing even one, and
always with the feeling of being seen by them all.
The rise and fall of the land the crooked path winding
through thick alders, never entering deeply,
never having it all. But what's so terrifying
except if your sense of self depends somehow
on the need for instrumental control on yourself
and your world? Was ownership and property
the only way to save the sense
of stability and order,
not accepting the inherent stability
of what a person is,
no different from that tiny waterfall

While looking out at the Bay

running through

rocks and moss, catching the evening

sunlight?

There never was a wilderness.

And so this land, Mi'kma'ki, was taken, measured and sold,

taken by force, force, with a realm of its own, laws of its own,

the laws of force. As Mother Ann Lee, founder of the Shakers.said,

every force evolves a form.

Arthur Bull

While looking out at the Bay

Waves

The oil tanker eventually and imperceptibly disappears,
its absence still changing the Bay and how it looks.
There's no going back from what has happened here,
and no unknowing not even to the deep, pure,
terrible pleasure of the Sublime. I look across
the Bay and even abstraction fades. Those three bands
disappear, horizon's border, an even grey-blue haze,
wide middle band with its ruffled silk surface,
almost breaking out in whitecaps, roughening

Arthur Bull

the water into feather-white patterns, and the nearest,
breaking in lacy waves, edging the rocky shore.
Now all three bands and all abstraction dissolve
into rhythm and movement, advance and retreat
of waves, each one a moving shape, a medium
for the transport of energy. Each wave passes by,
and appears to be going forward relentlessly,
while every water particle will stay in its place
only moving around the diameter of its circle.
Each particle moves on the diameter of this circle.
at the surface, equal to its wavelength. Large waves travel
seven kilometres an hour, while turning in vertical
orbits. New waves, approaching
the shore, have steeper
crests and troughs that flatten and broaden
into broader and flatter troughs. The forward movement

While looking out at the Bay

of the water particles at the top of the waves is always greater
than the backward movement in the trough and orbits
gradually move forward, causing, together with the direction
of the wind, the water to move toward the shore, where it feels
the drag of the bottom.

Waves batter headlands, undercut
cliffs and grind up beach material, then spill into
breakers, their steep fronts plunging forward, then collapsing.
These wind waves appear random. Their heights,
durations and shapes hard to predict. Their growth, propagation
and decay, and whatever governs the interdependence
between flow quantities: water surface movements,
velocities and water pressure form stochastic patterns,
like the stochastic music of the Greek composer Xenakis,
random and non-deterministic, where the next state

Arthur Bull

of the environment is not fully determined by the previous one.

    That water does not go forward with the waves
    as they go forward seems to make no sense.
    It goes nowhere, only up and down against
    the seeming truth of what our eyes perceive.

    What's moving through is form that also moves
    through the ocean of our experience
    the waves themselves with no innate substance,
    even breaking on the shore, there's nothing saved.

    I look around: bookshelves, cassettes, guitars,
    computer, Turkish rug, calligraphy,
    my hands, my thoughts, these words I write, my breath

    Inseparable as waves from oceans. They are
    like whitecaps on the Bay, and now I see
    the waves also include my birth and death.

Just like waves in a boundless sea blown by powerful wind,

breakers in a vast expanse, they never for a moment cease,

While looking out at the Bay

in the Ocean of Alaya, stirred by the wind of externality,
wave after wave of consciousness breaks and swells again,
blue and red and every colour; milk and sugar
and conch shell fragrances, and fruits and flowers, the sun
and moon and the light like the oceans and its waves are neither separate
nor not separate. Seven forms of consciousness
rise together in the mind like the ever changing sea,
repository of consciousness, gives rise to different forms,
mind, will, consciousness.

These are different forms,
devoid of differences. No seer and thing
Seen. As the ocean and its waves cannot be divided,
the mind and forms of consciousness cannot be separated.
The sea of storehouse consciousness is permanently subsisting.
The wind of phenomenal realms stirs, so various consciousnesses

Arthur Bull

spring up, churning out like waves. The way in which the sea gives
rise to the waves is the way in which the seven
consciousnesses rise inseparably from and with the eighth
storehouse: consciousness. Just as the sea agitates and the various
waves swell, so too the seven consciousnesses come about,
not different from the mind. And surface shifting
like tectonic plates darker bluer interacting
with lighter, ridges a fine white and rising along
the shore, a countermovement to the rows of waves.
This is the tide.

Looking , something caught my eye.
Further out, moving up and down on the waves,
lobster buoys dotting the water with no pattern, each one's
colours signifying whose they are. Orange with green stripe,

While looking out at the Bay

blue and white, half-yellow and half-blue,
solid red, red with double stripe, the colours say
not just who owns the buoy itself, but also who "owns"
this spot for the rest of the season. A claim made
and understood by all the others, a language not exactly
of ownership, but a mark of 'property' where the thing
that's owned is hard to see and fully understand.

So who owns what, then? What is a property? What
is belonging (or even longing)? And why does property
also refer to an attribute of something, or a predicate—
the property of him, a property of it? The buoys,
each point to the sentence 'This is his', describing
an attribute of his fishing activity that season.
But not in law, only in custom. In law it is the Crown's.
So property begins to refract, is in fact a prism

Arthur Bull

that refracts identity, the two being almost inseparable.
A fish dragger steaming along mid-bay is said
to own a quota, say, or rather the boat's owner does,
which is the legal right to catch some amount of fish,
so the access to the the ocean now becomes a product,
bought, sold, bequeathed and divided in divorce settlements,
a tangible abstraction, an attachment. This is a version
of market abstraction favoured by governments for its
elegance and simplicity, the way it cuts across complex
patterns of cooperation, unspoken communication
that form identities. Property and identity, closely interwoven,
standing still and moving, ephemeral and full of meaning.

Teachers sometimes use a floating piece of wood to illustrate
wave motion and non-motion. The attachment that property
has to the flow of energy is a form of communication

While looking out at the Bay

embedded in the wave, going forward and staying in place.
This is the same as radio waves, where the pattern
of a low frequency sound signal modulates the pattern
of a high frequency carrier signal so that a wave "carries"
information by the principle of modulation. The superimposition
of the sound signal of the message on the carrier signal
creates a third wave with a distinctive amplitude.

A property is an attribute, a predicate, bobbing on the waves.
Some say there are a numberless subjects and predicates,
all interacting in a beautiful system of ecological relation,
others say there is only one subject for all existing predicates.
Still others say that there are no predicates and there is no
subject, and neither is there the absence of any subject,
and neither is there the absence of any predicate.

Arthur Bull

I keep on looking out at the Bay. The waves keep on moving and staying still, whitecaps as far as the eye can see.

While looking out at the Bay

Currents

> *The problem is not how to stop the flow of items*
> *in order to stabilize space, but how to articulate*
> *the politics of the passage.*
> *- Lisa Robertson*

You can tell what's happening with the currents by the shapes water

makes, gliding on the surface of the Bay, slight differentiations

of blue-greys, sliding over each other like tectonic plates,

then closer into the shore, a satiny silvery ribbon,

smoother, holding sunlight, not sparkling like in rough

waters, but a longer shimmering layer of light, out

between the near and far Bay, mid-distance darker

Arthur Bull

mottled with deep blue, moving occasionally in slow
swirls tracing deeper currents and different temperatures.
Further out to the horizon, finer, lighter blues
infused with white reaching to grey streaked with rougher
surface. Gradually the wind crosses the Bay, moving
a fog bank folding in a common surface of grey,
erasing the three flowing bands with one single pooling
surface, smoothing over and over always shifting
in reciprocity with the other surfaces, always spreading
and holding the contract between smooth and ruffled,
then opening to show how the tide runs sometimes parallel
to the shore, sometimes in and out. Currents
where invisible forces of wind and deep sea become
visible, folding and unfolding, expressions, upwellings
and downdrafts, crosswinds, breaking in on themselves
like a language, solving and dissolving in the pattern

While looking out at the Bay

of change in one flow, all of the parts of the entire
belong to one organic whole, all interacting
as participants in one spontaneously self-generating process,
with no distinction between natural and human,
observer and observed, inner and outer. Everything
part of one single, collective, unending dance,
sometimes carrying bits of wood and debris, sometimes
islands of rockweed and sea wrack. The currents are the medium
of exchange for the Bay, carrying anything that goes in the water
to a new destination.
A Passamquoddy Chief told me once
that they used to put a canoe in the water at Gull Rock
near Grand Manan, 40 kilometres away, on a clear day
and ride the current that goes in a gyre around the middle
of the bay, and end up near Digby Gut.

Arthur Bull

The only way to cross the Bay of Fundy in a canoe
would be to know how to read the currents, which was how
Louis Jeremy did it back then, a Mi'kmaq man who lived
with his family in the Annapolis Valley. Well-liked
and respected in his time, he often provided firewood
and moose meat to neighbours in times of need. One fall
a busybody reported him to the game official for killing
an antlerless moose out of season. He could afford neither
the fine nor the jail term so he left, taking his family,
and canoed across the Bay, to New Brunswick and eventually
to Maine where he spent the rest of his life. The story
goes that he did return once to his place in Nova Scotia
and, again, he did this by paddling right across the Bay.

Currents are not random. They always go to the same places
in patterns, the visible signs of the wind, and movement

While looking out at the Bay

of water deep below. What is between these invisible forces
making both visible. asking and answering in patterns
of error and correction, syntax and grammar, nothing else?
"Things" are constituted of change not objects ever apart,
processes and relations operating within fields
that constitute structured systems. Things are made up of other
things that we can only understand by analyzing dialectic processes.
My horizon is a function of ecological and economic processes,
setting borderlines on space and time, not absolute, but multiple
produced parts and wholes are mutually constitutive,
Seen as both subjects and objects, transformative
action arises out of internal contradictions. Change
is characteristic of all systems. Observers are part
of the system as well as theories and possible worlds
constant process of actualization of possibilities.
Images present us with visual and emotional contradictions.

Arthur Bull

      Caught in between
      basalt boulders
      a child's plastic
                    flip-flop, turquoise.

Ocean currents are vehicles for the exchange of meaning.
Not random but following paths again and again, a medium
for whatever the ocean has gathered, it distributes it
in the same way unseen. I heard it said that,
if a fishermen drowns off Meteghan, his body
will usually be found in a particular cove on Digby Neck
But all I can read is what they bring, what they leave
behind, scattered along the shore: oil cans,
buoys, a child's turquoise shoe and, most strangely,
a basketball somehow stuck up into a tree. Some coves
and inlets seem to be destinations, gathering places

While looking out at the Bay

for storm toss and debris. About half a kilometre to the west,

Tar Cove, where Leify lived, was one of these.

I wrote a poem about it a few years ago.

Tar Cove

"The British Museum has lost its charm"
Ira Gershwin, A Foggy Day

What Tar Cove holds
is what's washed up.
A little sea of driftwood
white as bone,
of oil cans, faded
buoys, clumps of rope,
an orange glove,
a child's shoe,
a beam with giant bolts,
an iron bar,
twisted like a lasso, stencilled lettering
Amritsar-Calcutta,
a broken sea chest,

Arthur Bull

embossed in bronze
eyebrows, an ox head lyre,
a Maori tiki,
a necklace made
from the seals of Nineveh,
the Portland vase,
a swimming reindeer
scratched into a mammoth tusk,
the autograph manuscript
of *Kublai Khan*
complete with
uncompleted lines
sentences which should
have been said
but weren't,
forgotten phone numbers,
useless attachments
of every kind,
all might-have-beens
and rehearsals for
cancelled productions.
Lower the curtains.
Fade the lights.
Evening is coming

While looking out at the Bay

    to draw the covers
    over the waves
    along Tar Cove.

This ravelling and unravelling that delivers anything

to a new place happens not just in water, but everywhere.

The shoreline is a zone where everything mixes.

Animals also move along the rocky shore, open for walking.

Once I saw a big buck standing on an outcrop of rock

and there are signs of others, like coyote and lynx scat.

And once I had a much closer encounter with coyotes here.

I was sitting on the shore as I often did that summer

in a place sheltered between three big boulders,

a natural sitting place, where I had put a little platform

made of driftwood boards. I would take a few books

to read, a notebook and thermos of tea and a harmonica,

Arthur Bull

a Hohner 20-hole chromatic in case I felt like playing a tune.
Suddenly from around one of the boulders a coyote appeared,
trotting along, surprisingly big, with a beautiful
tawny coat. We were both shocked. It took off
but not far away, stopping at a little scraggly spruce,
and started to bark and yap, making a terrible racket,
but keeping there behind the little tree. Not knowing
what this might mean, and not sure just how to react
I instinctively reached for my harmonica and played a note,
and then another, slowly making it in to a little tune.
Then, from somewhere behind me, but not far away
came the sound of three or maybe four more coyotes singing
in a wolf-like harmony. I stopped playing, surprised
by the combined beauty of their voices, the unexpectedness
of this sound and how near they appeared to be.
They stopped singing, not more than half a minute

While looking out at the Bay

And without thinking why, I played another note,
and this time held it longer. When I stopped they began again
this time with a new chord, and so I held for a longer time.
We went back and forth like this for what seemed like minutes,
but in truth I have no idea l how long it was. The lone
coyote behind the tree kept yelping, so a kind of concerto
form, with call and response, started. Then, just
as suddenly as they started, they stopped, and the one in front
ran off down the shore. I do not know what it means.

Does it have to mean something? It feels like it should, perhaps
about the importance of music for all species, or the harmony
between people and nature, or possibility that they were just checking
me out as potential prey, and confused by the signal of my music.
The meaning probably does not matter in the end, just the story.
And the fact that it happened. Like so many stories this one

Arthur Bull

is probably about identity, the self, and how it can
even exist at all, not like it is a matter of fact or necessity at all.

Zhuangzi has lots to say about identity and how it changes.
Like the old men, old friends, who were comparing their situations.
One fell ill, and said, "Great is the Maker who has made me
as I am! I am so doubled up my guts are over my head.
My cheek rests on my navel. My shoulders stand out
beyond my neck. My crown is an ulcer surveying the sky.
My body is chaos but my mind is in order." Seeing his reflection
in a well, he said, "What a mess nature has made of me."
His friend asked, "Are you discouraged?" "Not at all!
Why should I be?" he answered. "If it takes me apart
and makes a rooster of my left shoulder I shall announce
the dawn. If it makes a crossbow of my right shoulder,
I shall get some roast duck. If my ass turns into a wheel,

While looking out at the Bay

and if my spirit is a horse, I will hitch myself up
and ride around in my own wagon! There is a time
for putting together, and another time for taking apart.
If you understand this you can meet each new state
in its proper time with neither sorrow nor joy."

All up and down the shore you can see driftwood
that the currents have carried here, each piece
a complete work, shaped by an artist, fit for some
Song poet's study, white and dry and unique
and completely unimportant to the ecology of the Bay
and the shore, just there, just purely ornamental.

Arthur Bull

While looking out at the Bay

Horizon

The eye lifts and follows the long view across the Bay
to the horizon, a limit clearly drawn out now, the Wolves
well out of sight, the furthest you can see from here. No more
oil tankers, gypsum boats, or scallopers. The longer
your eyes hold it there, the further your understanding
recedes from it. The limit before which everything
before it wants everything. Where all sight lines
meet and all limits merge into a single limit,
the furthest of everything—limit of view, limit of understanding,
limit of identity. When this happens, the horizon becomes

Arthur Bull

orizon kuklos, the separating circle. What's always there:
as far as you can see from where you are.

And that, the 'from where you are', is important, because
you are neither everywhere or anywhere, but only where
you are as much as you would want to be either,
or kid yourself that you are, or you are not, and you are not
nowhere either as much as you would like to think
you are, you're not, even if you have committed yourself
to a profession that claims to have the view from nowhere.

Looking out over the Bay, there is just one straight line,
and one thing alone that is completely unequivocal,
without equal, that beyond which you cannot see.
It's hard to admit your experience should be circumscribed
this way, a line drawn around your knowledge, but a relief

While looking out at the Bay

in a way. The question is: Can I change? Or are we fixed within our horizons without any capacity to understand the other person's world within their separate horizons?

The discovery of perspective, seeing that any line stands at the intersection and crossing of countless lines converging making visible a field of force known as space, receding in the distant meeting of heaven and earth, a boundary, a horizontal plane where all lines meet creating the illusion of depth. Gadamer says this about the possibility of the fusion of horizons":

> *Every finite present has its limitations.*
> *We define the concept of "situation" by saying*
> *that it represents a standpoint that limits*
> *the possibility of vision. Thus the essential*
> *part of the concept of "situation" is the*
> *concept of "horizon". The horizon*
> *is the range of vision that includes everything that*

Arthur Bull

can be seen from a particular vantage point: Person A and Person B exchange ideas and opinions within a conversation. People come from different places, have different opinions and this difference in background creates a set of prejudices and biases which provides various intrinsic values and meanings while the conversation is carrying on. By receiving the information from person A, a fusion of Person B's vision limitation is taking place and consequently it broadens Person B's range of horizon.

Horizon: the apparent line that separates earth from sky, the line

that divides all visible directions into two categories,

those that intersect the earth's surface and those that do not.

For navigation, before radio waves, it was the maximum

range of vision, and the only way to know where

you were.

In 1999 following the Supreme Court Marshall Decision

that recognized the rights of the Mi'kmaq, Maliseet and Passamaquoddy to participate in the commercial fishery, there was a conflict between Indigenous and non-Indigenous fishermen on the East Coast. In northern New Brunswick this resulted in serious violence, but in southwest Nova Scotia there was the potential of even greater violence. But it didn't happen. This story is about why it didn't happen.

In a moment when horizons changed, a moment of transformation. The crisis reached the point where there were six or seven hundred non-Native fishing boats tied up in Yarmouth harbour, ready for a violent confrontation with the Mi'kmaw fishing boats that were actively fishing in St. Mary's Bay about 30 kilometres away, fishing in the off-season. This crisis reached a point where it was clear they were close to large scale violent confrontation. Both sides were heavily armed, most of them also deer hunters

Arthur Bull

with high-powered rifles, and mostly very good shots.

At the peak of this tension there was a meeting
in Yarmouth with more than 500 fishermen with their reps.
They told the reps they would give them one more chance
to negotiate, to go and meet with the Chiefs from two bands in the area
and try one last time to find an agreement and if that don't work
'We're gonna take this into our own hands,' which meant
steaming up the bay and removing the Mi'qmaw boats by force.

This was on a Tuesday night in Yarmouth, and so a meeting
was set up. On Thursday morning the meeting convened
with just the fisherman's representatives and the Chiefs—
no press, no lawyers, no government, no mediators—
in a secret location.
They gathered there, the fishermen's reps and one of the Chiefs,

While looking out at the Bay

Deborah Robinson from the Acadia First Nation, but the other
Chief, Frank Meuse from the Bear River First Nation,
didn't show up, making for a very awkward and uncomfortable time
of waiting and difficult small talk. They really didn't say very much
at all, everybody knowing how high the stakes were,
how much pressure there was on everybody, and eventually,
more than an hour late, Chief Meuse arrived, and we saw
that he was holding an eagle feather. When he sat down
he said, 'I'd like to ask your permission to do something
different in this meeting.' He asked that the meeting
be held as a talking circle, and that
the eagle feather would pass around the circle,
and each person would speak only when he or she held
the eagle feather. Then he said the second part of his request:
that people wouldn't speak for themselves, but instead
for their grandfathers or grandmothers, imagining what

Arthur Bull

one of their grandfathers or grandmothers would say on that day.

So the feather went around and people spoke for their grandfathers and grandmothers. They spoke about the most personal experiences of growing up, of difficult times. Some spoke of poverty, some of pain, but all seemed to be picturing the face of one of their grandparents and it changed the way they spoke. At one point or other everybody in the room broke down in tears, sometimes moved beyond words the overwhelming feelings they were experiencing and by the emotions that were being shared around the circle, all the way around.
It took a long time, even though there were only a handful of people, because everyone spoke at length.

When the eagle feather came back
to Chief Meuse, he said, "I'd like to ask that the eagle feather
go around again because we need to go deeper than that,"

While looking out at the Bay

and everyone agreed. It went around again, and the second time
it took even longer and was even more moving for everyone.

Finally it came back to Chief Meuse again, and by this time people
had really got to know each other. Everyone stood up.
Some people hugged. We all felt very much closer
to each other than at the beginning. But then somebody said,
"Wait. We haven't talked at all about the fishery. We haven't
even begun to solve the problem of the lobster fishery—
what the fishermen are waiting for." So we sat back down,
and in less than 15 minutes worked out the complete solution
to the conflict, and ways that the First Nations fishermen could come
into the fishery: where they would get the licenses, how many traps
they would have, when they would fish and so forth, and every aspect
of the agreement. Then again they got up to leave and then Chief Meuse
went away and somehow came back with a roll of paper towels

Arthur Bull

and some crayons and asked everybody to join in,
to make a multicoloured banner with one word on it:

PEACE

The fishermen's meeting was the next night in Yarmouth.
It was packed with fishermen waiting to hear what had been decided.
All their representatives were there on the stage, and
Chief Deborah Robinson joined them. When she walked out on the stage
in front of hundreds of fishermen, they all stood and gave her a standing
ovation.

The story goes on in many ways from there,
and there were lots of lots of issues yet to be resolved,
and lots of negotiation. It was not the end of the conflict,
but it was a turning point, a watershed. As a result,

While looking out at the Bay

there followed many collaborations and joint projects.
But mostly violence was averted because of a breakthrough,
a transformational moment of meeting in a different way.
Maybe this is an example of Gadamer's fusion of horizons.

Each of us has a horizon, made by history because we are historical
beings. Each one's limit is given by our place and the people
before and around us, with whom we find ourselves
living our lives. The line we cannot see beyond
that we cannot see. And yet our lives, if they are to be more
than just living, must find a way to see beyond
our horizons, and fuse with the horizons of the other.
We must some how hold our horizons lightly, and ready
to change with them when they meet with difference.
We must be willing to accept that the absolute certainty
we feel about our horizons, and the identities they give us

Arthur Bull

are not in fact absolute at all, while at the same time
being the mark of our possibilities they are the certainty
of our limits. And this must be the real possibility
of becoming human in the recognition that every one
of us is defined by our absolute finitude and that, that,
is the common horizon that we all share. What we
occasionally get a glimpse of when we happen to meet.

The truth is that there is just one horizon, our common limit.

While looking out at the Bay

Seaweed

> *In all parts of the world a rocky and*
> *partially protected shore perhaps supports*
> *a given space with a greater number*
> *of individual animals than any other station.*
> *- Charles Darwin*

Where the water and land meet there is a constant rhythm of exchange.

The steady rolling movement of seaweed back and forth

is rhythm's rise and fall, always measuring movement

of water, making visible the invisible pattern of tide

and current moving, but at the same time not moving, attached

by its holdfast on the rocks. Undulating rhythm, repetitions

Arthur Bull

of motion and time, and never in exact repetitions, the slow
back and forth on the swell and stream that keeps repeating,
but never in exact series. It is the differences, disruptions
and disjunctions that happen between each moment and movement
as it repeats that makes rhythm: Frond and thallus,
cryptogam and phanergams, thallophytes and compytes, leaf
and stem swaying together like ballroom dancers dancing
to a silent orchestra.

An aside: what would your old Canadian poets
have to say about seaweed? Typically he, say Bliss Carman, would say
with a lyrical surge, how it is born on gigantic storm-wind
toiling swells, sea-laden rocks, outpouring then he'd
go far away to distant lands, preferably warm:
Bermuda, say, or the Azores, Bahamas, San Salvador,
anywhere tropical and exotic, predicting our need

While looking out at the Bay

today to go south to the all-inclusives in winter.
Then northward to harsh and poetic places: Orkneys,
Hebrides, desolate, more like home, but perhaps
a little more rugged and manly. Then he would, maybe,
upping the ante, go travelling away to higher concepts:
Truth, Heaven, Youth, Will, Fate, Endeavor,
and having called up the great ideas he then
finds himself worried again by some sense of unease.
His restless heart is really what is drifting on the currents,
shifting all the time even to the point of waste
and desolation.

Here is the nub of the matter. What is in fact bothering the poet,
in spite of all the previous attempts at distraction,
so carefully crafted in pentameter and rhyme?
Lacking an answer, I will only enumerate:

Arthur Bull

Sea lettuce, hollow greenweed, green cord, mermaid's hair,
horse tail sea sorrel, finger kelp, oarweed kelp,
sea colander, knotted wrack, rockweed, spiral wrack,
toothed wrack, whip weed, sea lichen, purple laver,
rosy laver, dulse, Irish moss, sea paint brush, sea bag,
curled weed, stone strub, red crust,
fronds filliform, branched tufts, flabellate anadymen,
rigid memranaceous surface, network of veins, merman's
shaving brush, whirls of branchlets each overlapping
the previous rockweeds, sucker-like discs olive green,
oarweed's devil's apron, sole leather sea furbelows,
green rope, red threadweeds gelatinous, leafweed,
callithamnium, pither weeds, ulvaria dulse wire, weed tubed
seaweed, red fern, sea paintbrush, sea hag,
sea oak, brown featherbush, sea beard,
ribbon weeds, finger kelp, oarweed, knotted wrack ,

While looking out at the Bay

whip weed, sea lichen, sausage weed, sea potato.

The interaction between place, time, the expenditure of energy,
and rhythm of capital producing and destroying the rhythm of life.
What does it reify, how does it become embodied in a body?
How does it replace necessity, replace love and pleasure,
the body carried on the great rhythms of historical time.
The history of rhythm, or the rhythm of history,
enacts itself on a concept of life and the body, the time
of living. The tragic simulates life with rhythms as sameness
and difference combining polyrhymicalities.

The sounds
of the Bay: wind, waves, birds, breathing, heartbeat,
silences between sounds,. Secret rhythms, public rhythms,
fictional rhythms, dominating rhythmic, the triad

Arthur Bull

of isorhythmic, eurhythmic, arrhythmic movement,
of geological time, basalt time, kalpas
not in the sense that there is identical rhythm. There must
be difference always moving together with sameness.
Starting with waves, then working outward until you reach
everyday rites, ceremonies, rules, laws, all the rhythms
of social time and space, even the transformation of nature
through labour, of capital producing and destroying erects
itself on its contempt for life, the body and rhythm of leisure.

The rhythmanalysis of place always begins with the body,
tides sluicing the blood back and force through arteries;
the hiss of the surf in your ear (if you have tinnitus, as I do);
winds lifting and dropping the lungs like the waves
over the depths; even your thoughts moving like the currents
sometimes breaking the surface, often just barely present,

While looking out at the Bay

invisible and beyond hearing, the part of the rhythm
that is unknown, unseen, unheard, but still there.

There is an elementary exercise used in teaching tabla
That demonstrates that a beat, a measure of duration in time,
can be filled with sound in an infinite number of ways. It is not
the sound you make when you clap your hands
or hit the drum. That is just a marker to show the beginning
of the duration in time that is the beat. The exercise goes like this.
Start a medium tempo rhythm and divide it in eight
equal parts, and say them out loud, repeating it:
one, two, three, four, five, six, seven, eight.
Then say it but keep the one silent: two, three, four,
five, six, seven, eight, then keep the one and two silent:
three, four, five, six, seven, eight. Continue until one
to eight are all silent, then work backwards.

Arthur Bull

The beat is not the sound, but a measure of time divided by sounds.

Rhythm combines the
heard and unheard,
visible and invisible, being and becoming,
clay and flesh,
life and death, noun and verb,
known and unknown,
the sameness and difference
fit together to manifest
the beat, and bring us to
the one beat, the single rhythm,
without beginning or end.

While looking out at the Bay

Clouds

After the long walk through the dark woods,
down steep gullies, across mud holes,
climbing over fallen trees, past shadows
of mossy erratics, path closed in by spruce and alder,
suddenly and without warning I arrive high above
the shore. At that very same moment there appears
the sky, today a perfectly sky blue as far
as I can see above, away, beyond, open,
but not empty, because moving through it
are massive shifting cumulus clouds, rising

Arthur Bull

dragon shapes with lightly shaded lower edges,
torn along their tops like construction paper,
or coral, or basalt, or scholar stones, their sides,
shape-shifting in all directions, slow moving
separate continents of white transient energy.

That is what this chapter is about. In particular
about how clouds are at the same time so complete
and well-formed while being so temporary and insubstantial
as we mean when we use 'nebulous'
to describe an opinion or attitude that lacks definition
or substance. Or what Aristophanes meant
when he called Socrates' ideas no more than clouds.
But the question is this: What do we do
in the face of this seeming contradiction when we
are looking up at clouds in the sky above us?

While looking out at the Bay

One of the first things we like to do is put clouds
into categories. Luke Howard did this in 1802
in his essay *On the Modification of Clouds,* which proposed
a system of classification that the whole world uses to this day.
Not only those domed heaps of cumulus that I see now
with their flat, wide forms, rising as unstable energies,
but also all the rest I remember floating over the Bay:
dense ribbed blankets of rolling stratocumulus,
hazy sheets of stratus indefinite covering everything
(that when they come down become the fog we're in)
cirrus's feathery brushstrokes, called mares' tails (why mares?),
layered ripples of cirrocumulus in mackerel back,
thin veils of cirrostratus drawing delicate detail,
the dull grey of altostratus blocking out the sun,
towers of altocumulus rising up into the blue,
and heavy nimbus rainclouds weighed down,

Arthur Bull

or starting as cumulonimbus that lift and swell,
violent vertical black anvil shaped thunderclouds
or nimbostratus dense rainclouds filling the sky.
Then all the species of form and structure that
each kind takes: smooth, fibrous, ragged, tufted,
broken, dense, tubular, torn, hooked, layered.
Then all varieties of transparencies and arrangements:
tangled, curved, net-like, radiating, thick, arched,
towering, ribbed, fishbone-like, hooded, translucent.
And then there's all the ways the categories combine
like the single delicate wisp of cirrus that hangs
in front of the cumulus, or the dark shadowy bank
of cumulonimbus that glowers to the west over Grand Manan.
And this is to say nothing of all the ways
that the cloud categories change into each other.

While looking out at the Bay

When talking about categories, we have to bring in Aristotle,
the master-sorter who had a basket for everything
and put everything in a basket so well that we
kept them there for two thousand years. They came in handy,
starting with, first, the Said-of and Present–In,
then second to the Not Said-Of and Present-In,
followed by the third, the Not-Said-Of and Not-Present-In,
and don't forget the fourth, Said-Of and Not-Present-In,
which he then sorted into a tenfold division including
substance, quality, relativeness, and quantity.

As well as categorizing, we like to explain why they are
and how they come about, when we look at clouds.
Something about cooling, how moist, saturated air
condenses by mixing with another body of cooler air,
or by forcing over mountains or heavier air,

Arthur Bull

and how it must have something to condense on:
small particles of sulphur or nitrogen compounds
or sea-salt particles, the density of which depends
on the velocity of the wind, nearness of oceans or smoke, and
temperature. And so the explanation goes from here.

What this gives us is all the facts and occurrences
that accompany and cause clouds, without really
telling us anything about our question: impermanent
and well-formed bodies that we see both at once.

Another response is to see things in clouds the way
people like to see things in abstract paintings—
a horse, a hand, a sunset, a roast of beef—
projecting whatever configurations of their desires
they call up from the theatre of their culture,

While looking out at the Bay

anything rather than just looking at the painting

and experiencing anything even slightly unfamiliar,

or abstracted from the forces of need and want.

Yet another response to seeing such passing beauty

is of course to create more beauty and more clouds

There is so much writing about how to do this.

In 1785 Alexander Cozens in *A New Method of Assisting*

Invention in Drawing Original Compositions of Landscape

says,

> To...sketch is to transfer ideas from the mind to the paper,
> producing accidental forms, from which ideas are presented...
> To sketch is to delineate ideas; blotting suggests them.

The Mustard Seed Garden Manual of Painting (1679)

describes the large hook outline, one of the two main ways

Arthur Bull

to paint clouds:

> *washes of pure colour should be applied*
> *...and should show no traces of ink.*

and goes on to say,

> *[This] should show no traces of ink, light ink*
> *for outlining and light wash of pale blue for tinting.*

The other is the small hook or outline style,

which is about using line rather than colour for clouds.

Painters and critics have spilled centuries of ink

about which was the better way to paint clouds.

The book also says

> *Clouds are the ornaments of sky and earth,*
> *the embroidery of mountains and streams.*

While looking out at the Bay

> *They may move as swiftly as horses.*
> *They may seem to strike a mountain with such force*
> *that one almost hears the sound of the impact.*

As for painting them it goes on to say

> *First in vast landscapes of numerous cliffs and valleys*
> *clouds were used to divide (and hide) parts of the scene.*
> *Richly verdant peaks soared into the sky and*
> *white scarves of clouds stretched horizontally*
> *separated and imprisoned them.*

All this reminds me of

clouds around Prince Rupert, where I worked years ago,

the unmoving cirrus clouds that always wreathed the mountains

that I wrote this poem about.

Arthur Bull

                        wispy clouds

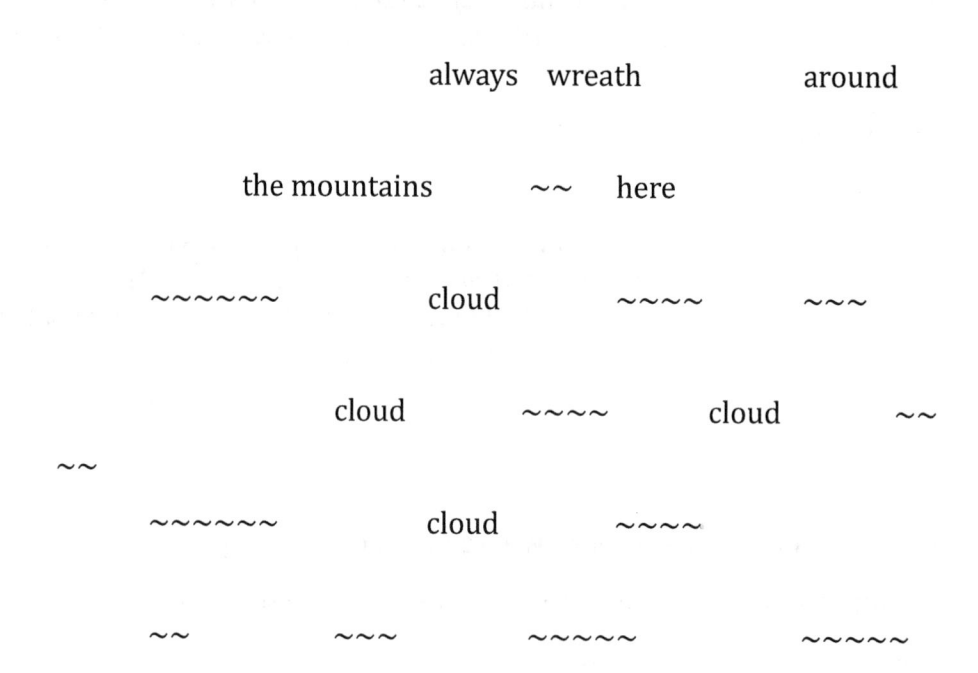

                              always   wreath   around

                the mountains   ~~   here

      ~~~~~   cloud   ~~~~   ~~~

                  cloud   ~~~~   cloud   ~~

~~

      ~~~~~   cloud   ~~~~

  ~~   ~~~   ~~~~~   ~~~~~

The mountainous cumulus clouds have darkened and now are moving fast across the sky above the Bay.

While looking out at the Bay

Faced with this dynamic change we can also reflect on the nature of change and in particular, the relationship between beauty and justice. The struggle for social change, whether won or lost, entails coming to terms with the nature not only of nature, but of human society. Facing beauty in nature seems, in our common understanding, quite separate from the beauty of justice and the great movement that creates it.

But why? As Weil puts it, to see beauty is "to give up our imaginary position as the centre….a sensibility that takes place at the very roots of our sensibility." And this is the same shift that underlies our sense of justice.

Years ago I was involved in the movement of inshore fishermen against the privatization

Arthur Bull

of their fishery, and the loss of their communities,

the ocean being the last great frontier for capitalism.

I wrote this poem about what happened.

End of the Rope March, February 1996

The weather that day was anything but
beautiful, worst blizzard in years,
but they drove through it to Halifax

From every corner of the province
to walk the streets of the capital, holding
onto a rope, inshore fishermen and their families,
more than five thousand they say,
that came out that February day—

From Advocate Harbour, from Englishtown, from Westport,
Lockport, Meteghan, from Clark's Harbour,
Tancook, from Pinkney's Point, Victoria Beach,
from Freeport, Centreville, Harbourville, Arisaig,
from Port Maitland, from Ecum Secum,

While looking out at the Bay

from Canso—from everywhere small boats
set out in stormy waters to make a livelihood fishing,

Holding a rope—along Barrington, along Granville,
through the Maritime Centre—holding a rope,
a metaphor that everyone understood:
'end of the rope.'

Nothing beautiful about why we were there:
big money wanting it, wanting them
out, invisible and silent and harsh
as harsh can be. Everyone knew
this rope was the same as the lines
that hold each boat—bow lines, stern lines, trap lines, gillnet
lines, trawl lines. And every place
had its own take

and its own say: my name became shibboleth,
with its hard 'r' and its 'th', so that
each time someone said hello
I heard the sweet vowels and consonants
that told of a place—'awtha' from Shelburne,
'aatha' from Bridgewater, 'artur' (like Newfoundland)
from Cape Breton, 'archer' from the French Shore,

Arthur Bull

    the unforgiving hard 'R' 'arrrthur'
    of Digby Neck, my home,

    So beautiful. There was nothing beautiful
    about what lay ahead: the total
    collapse of the handline fishery, the total loss,
    village by village, of a way of life
    relegated to history. So holding that rope,
    hands tiny and smooth or massive
    and calloused, we walked like a river of tears.
    We ribbonned through those city streets
    like a vein of agate through basalt,
    sun-glittering through grey, and that,
    that was beautiful.

Now, looking out at the Bay, all that seems so far

away, even though in a sense it was all about

the Bay itself. I watch the clouds roll over, and feeling

the changeability of everything I have experienced,

I chant the words of a sutra someone wrote long ago:

While looking out at the Bay

Form is nothing but emptiness, emptiness is nothing but form, form is exactly emptiness, emptiness is exactly form.

Arthur Bull

While looking out at the Bay

Fog again

> *Most of us live in two worlds—our real world*
> *and the one we build or spin for ourselves*
> *out of the books we read, the heroes we admire,*
> *the things we hope to do.*
> *Greta's other world was Blue Cove.*
> *Julia Sauer, "Fog Magic"*

Stratus is the one kind of cloud we can be inside of.

Now a grey layer has descended, enclosing the Bay,

and everything I have been looking out at: waves, currents,

seaweed, rocks, plants, horizon, other clouds.

Now with no sight, colour, shape or distance the mind falls

Arthur Bull

back into its own world. Voices begin to tell
their stories, sometimes as dreams, sometimes as the recurring
narratives we tell ourselves in order to be ourselves, or so
we like to think, and sometimes stories that were read
to us as kids, like *Glooscap Tales*, *Bluenose Ghosts*
and the best known book about this place, Digby Neck,
Fog Magic by Julia Sauer. She was a librarian from Rochester, NY
who spent her summers in Little River, just a ways
along the shore from here.

It's a young person's book,
a fantasy, set in the 1940s, about an eleven-year-old girl
named Greta Addington. It turns on the trope
that one child in every generation of Addingtons
can go back on foggy days to the turn of the century
to Blue Cove, an abandoned village that appears

While looking out at the Bay

in fair weather to be just some ruined foundations,
but when fog rolls in, comes alive with all its people.
She has a friend to play with there, whose family
says she has come to visit "from over the mountain".
Greta goes there on her twelfth birthday, and that night
in Blue Cove her friends give her a kitten, and Greta
leaves, realizing she will never be able to return.

Blue Cove is based on White's Cove, just over the mountain
from Little River. The real genius of the book is the telling
of stories that Sauer heard on her visits, stories inside the story,
stories that are still told on Digby Neck, even in the schoolyard.
Jerome the legless man who was found, on the beach
at Sandy Cove, unable to speak except for what sounded
like "Jerome", which became his name. That mystery
was never solved. A boulder on that beach is called

Arthur Bull

Jerome's Rock to this day. Or the young girl, the housekeeper
to an older man who one day accused her of stealing
his money. She ran off into the woods never to be seen
again, but appears to Greta in the woods at Blue Cove.
Or the woman who walked three hundred miles to Halifax
to seek justice from the government and get her land back,
which had been wrongly granted to someone else.
The book is filled the stories about and from this place.

The telling of stories is what makes a community
or what the Greeks called "polis". Arendt says,

> *Such a narrative, formulated within the network of human relations and destined for a political inter-esse, is fundamentally integrated into action and can demonstrate this essential logic only by itself becoming actions.*

While looking out at the Bay

Kristeva comments,

Arendt finds a community space made up of political perspectives that are in a way pre- and post-theoretical....

Stories contain

stories, and give rise to more stories

in a long series, the way clouds are always translating

from cumulus to stratus to cirrus, transforming themselves

continuously into each other. Stories give

birth to new stories. For example, the fact that Blue Cove

is based on White's Cove gives rise to the story

of the struggle about the quarry at White's Point,

located right beside it.

In 2002 an American-owned company,

Bilcon of Nova Scotia, proposed to build a quarry

Arthur Bull

there, one of the biggest on the eastern seaboard,
to export 40,000 tons of basalt every week.
The struggle to stop the quarry was long and hard,
starting with a petition signed by the vast majority
of Digby Neckers, followed by the creation of an alliance
of community associations, local agencies, environmental groups,
municipal government, fishermen's associations, local businesses,
Bear River First Nation and more. The opposition
was based on the threat the quarry presented to the lobster,
herring, scallop, urchin and other fisheries, the emergent
and successful whale watching industry and the potential
to become a major international ecotourism destination,
to the essential fresh water supply for the local fishplant,
the daily quality of life for inhabitants of Little River,
and to a community's ability to create its own future.

While looking out at the Bay

The struggle went on for five years. The company used
bribery, deceit, litigation, intimidation: the basic
toolbox of rural industrial development everywhere.

Finally, at a hearing, the alliance
spoke to the panel charged with
making the decision and, speaking in the ancient
language of supplication, beseeched the panel
to spare them a future at the mercy of this brutal company.

In the end we won. We stopped, the quarry. It left
the community divided, scarred and exhausted, but joined
with brothers and sisters around the world in resistance
struggles, as protectors of land and sea and livelihoods and places.

This is the paradigm of colonial natural resource development.

Arthur Bull

Fish, animals and trees long ago made into commodities
and stripped out, and now the very place, the rock we stand on
would be sold, leaving just another wasteland, and young men
drunk on a Saturday night with pockets full of cash.

Stories like this are collective, but then break apart
into our individual stories one after the other in rapid
succession. Ruth and I camping on the shore in a pup tent
right down on the rocks beside the waves, awakened
suddenly by a loud and strange bellowing sound:
two whales blowing and feeding right close beside us.
Did they know we were there? Do whales have stories?

Meeting other species is about stories too. Riopelle's
last works are all about animals, as are Char's poems
about the Lascaux animals, and the cave paintings themselves.

While looking out at the Bay

The fog stays and the stories fade, leaving only
the sound of the gulls against the wash of the surf,
and then slowly the sound of your breathing and
the beating of your heart, now with only sound
a new space begins to open out, free from what
happened next (...and then...and then...) and who did what.
Free and open, only space marked out by sparse sounds.

The first time I was aware of how this space
can open out was with the Great Black Music of the 60s.
Along with Albert Ayler's hymns to love, Coltrane's transcendent Africa,
Cecil Taylor's layers of poetic energy, there was another
music—*The Heliocentric World of Sun Ra*, sound by Roscoe Mitchell,
Milford Graves—music that opens up space and a kind of freedom
that in turn leads to a deep listening beyond the stories

Arthur Bull

of who we are supposed to be, the listening beyond, where we start to hear other species and other spirits.

That music led to other paths, the opening out of space punctuated with improvised sound, and to art that went beyond while staying completely present. Sun Ra says, "Space is not only high, it's low. It's a bottomless pit."

I wrote a poem years ago called *What They Are Giving for Today*

> "Spontaneity if the sign of generosity"
> Paul-Emile Borduas

> > Said somewhere in
> > Refus Global

> Enough, more than enough
> to spare: a plenitude

While looking out at the Bay

      Rain last night
      sun by midday

Inside, giving clarity
outside, movement

      Feng, the Arousing:
      Lightning and Thunder

Something in reserve
giving room to move around

      It will be enough
      to improvise

Arthur Bull

While looking out at the Bay

Tidepool

I turn my eyes from the white expanse of fog, downward
and there at my feet is a tidepool, a tiny world alive
with movement and colour, self-contained, giving life
to a world of names, fantastic and strangely well-suited
to this pool's miniature universe: zig-zag wine glass
hydroids, trumpet-stalked jellyfish, frilled anemone,
leafy and bristly bryozoa, white-slippered limpet,
periwinkle, sea spider, barnacles, sandhoppers,
copepods, sowbugs, starfish, sea palms, urchins,
sea cradles, moonsnails, and dragonflies.

Arthur Bull

While looking out at the Bay

Coda

Sea Beach Raga

There is no room in that huge meeting
of ocean sky and land
for anything less than the equation
permits: a sufficiency.
Turning away I said, here, that is enough.
But something turned me walking again
further along the shore to find
any tiny particulars as I went:
The dried black leather bubble
with four tails at the corners:
a mermaid's purse (imagine that!).
It is the egg case of a skate.

Arthur Bull

>The grantia cilianta (urn shaped
>or oval, large aperture at the summit)
>A sponge (surrounded by a circle
>of projecting spicules).
>And as I went something said more,
>there is more and afraid of what
>I had missed I kept on gathering
>and turning back a blanket of rockweed
>I found a sea cucumber (ovate body,
>pentagonal, a dark purple and white)
>I'd only seen them before in Chinatown
>pickled in baskets on the sidewalk
>(How wonderful to be alive at all,
>to have a body in this world!)
>Laminaria, oarweeds, tangle
>sole-leather and devil's apron
>until following the thread of each thing
>toward kingdom, branch, class, order,
>family, genus, species, memories,
>diaries, mistakes, letters and the wind,
>each like a nerve end filiating outward,
>and each end tracing the meandering line
>of the walk as I went, the shape of a melody
>as in the slow exposure of the raga,

While looking out at the Bay

each step leading from chance to attention
(until I arrived again and looked up
at that meeting of land and sky and ocean)
and something said finally yes that is enough

Arthur Bull

Mentors

Hannah Arendt
(1906–1975) Political philosopher, author, and Holocaust survivor. One of the most influential political theorists of the 20th century. Her writing on violence and trauma has been important to me in my political work.

Aristophanes
(c.446 – c.386 BC) Comic playwright in Ancient Athens and a poet of the Old Attic Comedy. He gets into this poem because of his play *The Clouds*, as much for the title as anything else.

Aristotle
(384–322 BC) Greek philosopher and polymath, probably the most influential of all Western philosophers. He wrote about logic, biology, literature, ethics, rhetoric, politics and much else, but not all at once.

Arthur Bull

Jean Arp
(1886–1966) German-French sculptor, painter, and poet. His works, although they are seen as part of the Dada movement, represent, in his own words, 'the secret life of nature.'

René Char
(1907–1988) French poet and member of the Resistance in World War II. His late series about animals depicted in the Lascaux caves have always affected me.

Alexander Cozens
(1717–1786) British watercolour landscape artist, wrote treatises on the subject, evolving a method in which imaginative drawings of landscapes could be worked up from abstract blots on paper. A painter well ahead of his time.

Charles Darwin
(1809–1882) English naturalist, geologist, biologist, founder of evolutionary biology. Darwin influenced everyone, but few have actually read his work. *The Voyage of the Beagle* is a literary classic.

Hans-Georg Gadamer
(1900–2002) German philosopher, best known for his magnum opus *Truth and Method*, about hermeneutics. I came to his work work through

an essay by Canadian philosopher Charles Taylor.

Luke Howard
(1772-1864) British manufacturing chemist and amateur meteorologist, who created the categorization of clouds we use today. Sometimes called 'The Godfather of Clouds', he is the patron saint of all non-academic researchers and intellectuals.

Karl Marx
(1818–1883) German philosopher, economist, historian, sociologist, political theorist, journalist, critic of political economy and socialist revolution. Comments about him often begin with, "Say what you will about Marx..." The lectures by British geographer David Harvey, best read over a pint in the pub opposite the British Museum, are a good introduction to Marx's *Capital*.

Henry Moore
(1898–1986) English artist, best known for his semi-abstract, monumental bronze sculptures which are located around the world as public works of art. His work is very present in Toronto at the Art Gallery of Ontario and several public locations, which oddly work somehow.

Mother Ann Lee
(1736–1784) Founder of the Shakers, a millenarian Christian movement. I

Arthur Bull

came to her through an essay by Guy Davenport.

Charles Sanders Peirce
(1839–1914) American philosopher, logician, mathematician and scientist, logician, mathematician and scientist, sometimes known as "the father of pragmatism".

Jean-Paul Riopelle
(1923–2002) Québecois painter and sculptor, known for his abstract painting style, in particular his "mosaic" works of the 1950s, when he famously abandoned the paintbrush, using only a palette knife to apply paint to canvas, giving his works a distinctive sculptural quality. One of my favourite art exhibitions of all time was the Riopelle/Mitchell, with his long-time partner and collaborator Joan Mitchell.

Lisa Robertson
(born 1961) Canadian poet, essayist and translator. Her subject matter includes political themes, such as gender and nation, as well as the problems of form and genre. Her exploration of literary forms such as the pastoral, epic, and weather forecast informed my approach to this poem.

Mark Rothko
(1903–1970) American abstract painter, best known for his colour field paintings that depicted irregular and painterly rectangular regions of

colour. The always-horizontal paintings kept coming to mind as I looked out at the Bay, so I had to bring him in.

Allan Sekula
(1951–2013) American photographer, writer, filmmaker, theorist and critic. He made us aware that the oceans are the basic medium of globalization of late capitalism.

J. M. W. Turner
(1775–1851) English Romantic painter and watercolourist, known for his expressive colourisations, imaginative landscapes and turbulent, dramatic marine paintings. John Ruskin's writing about the sublime took Turner's paintings as its starting point.

Simone Weil
(1909–1943) French philosopher, mystic and political activist. Her works, especially the essay *The Iliad—The Poem of* Force, are essential reading for our time.

Xenakis
(1922 – 2001) Greek-French composer, music theorist, architect, performance director and engineer. Pioneered the use of mathematical models in music, such as applications of set theory, stochastic processes and game theory; also an important influence on the development of electronic and

Arthur Bull

computer music. I have never performed his music, and don't understand the theory behind it, but I love how his music creates clouds of notes, like a murmuration of starlings.

Zhuangzi
(late 4th century BC) Influential Chinese philosopher who lived during the Warring States period in China. He is credited with writing—in part or in whole—a work known by his name, the *Zhuangzi*, which is one of the foundational texts of Taoism.

Acknowledgements

I would like to thank those early readers of the manuscript who gave me feedback and encouragement, including Maria Recchia, Hank Bull, Mary Bull, David Lee, Bill Smith, George Elliott Clarke, and Guy Ewing.

A note of much gratitude goes to Dr. Sherry Pictou, who generously loaned me the pamphlet *The Story of Louis Jeremy,* and without whose support and inspiration over the years this book would not have been written.

And special thanks to Moose House Publications, and to Andrew Wetmore for the care, attention and patience he brought to the editing process.

Arthur Bull

About the author

Arthur Bull lives in Lake Midway on Digby Neck, in Nova Scotia. He has previously published six books of poetry and five chapbooks, and his poems and translations from classical Chinese have appeared in numerous Canadian, US and international journals. He is also a musician and has been part of the improvised music scene in Canada for more than 40 years.

As a long-time activist he has worked primarily with small-scale fisheries organizations and rural development organizations at the local, national and international level.